Table of Contents

Start a dog training business by following these steps:

You have found the perfect business idea, and now you are ready to take the next step. There is more to starting a business than just registering it with the state. We have put together this simple guide to starting your dog training business. These steps will ensure that your new business is well planned out, registered properly and legally compliant.

Plan your Business

A clear plan is essential for success as an entrepreneur. It will help you map out the specifics of your business and discover some unknowns. A few important topics to consider are:

• What are the startup and ongoing costs?

- Who is your target market?

- How long it will take you to break even?

- What will you name your business?

Luckily we have done a lot of this research for you.

What are the costs involved in opening a dog training business?

The startup costs associated with opening a dog training business are relatively minimal. Business owners need to have a phone and computer so they can effectively communicate with clients and market online.

Aside from this, they either need a place to train dogs or transportation to clients' homes. Those who don't want to sign a long-term lease may be able to rent space a few days a week in a pet store, use a local park or train dogs in a fenced-in yard.

What are the ongoing expenses for a dog training business?

A dog training business has two primary ongoing expenses. Unless training dogs in a home, the business must continue to lease or rent space for training dogs. How much this cost amounts to depends on where the business is located, how much space it uses and how often the business uses the space. The business must also pay to renew any certifications that expire. Renewing certifications usually doesn't cost as much as initially becoming certified.

Who is the target market?

An ideal client is someone who has at least one dog, has discretionary income and is busy. People who have little discretionary income are less likely to pay someone to train their dog. People who have many obligations and discretionary income are less likely to have time to train their dog themselves and have income to pay a training business.

How does a dog training business make money?

Dog training businesses are paid for training dogs. Businesses may offer multi-week classes people can sign their dogs up for, one-on-one lessons and remedial behavior correction sessions. Additionally, some dog training businesses also offer dog walking, dog sitting and dog grooming, which provide additional income sources.

How much can you charge customers?

The cost of dog training varies widely, depending on a trainer's expertise, the number of dogs in a class and the location of a business. Group classes typically cost $50 to $125 and run between four and eight weeks. Private lessons typically range from $30 to $100 per hour, with most dogs requiring at least several hours of training. The higher ends of these ranges are usually earned by trainers who have at least one certification.

How can you make your business more profitable?

Dog training businesses can increase profits by opening more classes, encouraging people to sign up for individual sessions, getting trainers more certifications or adding other services. Starting more classes and signing clients up for one-on-one sessions increases how many hours dogs are being trained, and thus increases revenue. Getting more certifications gives trainers more expertise, allowing a business to charge more for the amount of time they spend training dogs. Adding other services, such as dog walking, dog sitting or dog grooming lets a business continue to serve clients after their dogs have been trained.

Being an entrepreneur isn't easy. It takes dedication, drive and passion for the industry you're going into as well as for the business itself. Many pet parents dream and ponder how to start a dog training business for many reasons, but the most common is a simple love for dogs and a desire to improve the relationship between pets and their owners.

Working with pets is a rewarding experience, and even more so when you can be your own boss: planning, creating, imagining and implementing everything from A to Z. If this sounds like you, and you believe you're a hard working enough person with an interest in dog training, the first step to figuring out exactly how to start a dog training business is to actually commit to this venture.

Keep in mind though that regardless of the sense of adventure, excitement and optimism that will come once you take your first steps into building your own dog training business, it will not always be an easy road to travel. In fact, pet parents who are dead set on launching a dog training business should prepare for a long road of many hours and hard work.

"30% OF NEW BUSINESSES IN THE USA FAIL WITHIN THE FIRST TWO YEARS AFTER LAUNCH…"

…according to the US Small Business Administration; and within the first five years that number can jump up to a 50% failure rate. Although this is true across all industries, not just pet businesses, the failure rate in running a dog training business specifically can be even higher for many different reasons.

Always begin with learning as much as you can and research of the industry you're about to enter.

Doing your homework before you begin – along with plenty of investigation of what's out there – will definitely and significantly improve the odds of your dog business becoming successful. You'll also want to make sure that you have a good support system set up around you, because starting a business, no matter what kind, is a very stressful undertaking overall.

What do I mean by "support system"? It's the people and the environment that surrounds you: avoid all the negativity and consume all positive thoughts and encouragement from those who push you into learning how to start a dog training business. Additionally, gather around all types of resources for information and reference. Grab dog business books, subscribe to our newsletter and follow our Dog Business Column.

"I'm ready. I can do this. I'm dedicated and I want to learn how to start a dog training business!"

First thing's first...

Dog training industry is competitive. But what's even more important to know is that it's also unregulated, meaning that anyone can be a dog trainer, even without any dog training certifications. Some dog owners may hire trainers who are not qualified in the least to train a canine. Thus it's important to get unbiased, objective opinions of your dog training knowledge and handling skills from third-party sources (preferably NOT your family and friends).

If you haven't already done anything like that, make sure to take group classes or private lessons with your own dog in learning how to train dogs professionally. We even have a great column on how to get a dog trainer's certification, if you wish to look into that.

To make sure that your dog training business stands out from the crowd, you'll want to have as many canine training skills on your resumé as possible. Take additional classes and seminars that offer more certificates of completion, new skills, ideas, and if possible, get a list of references of people that have seen your ability to train dogs first-hand.

Having a huge crush on dogs does not qualify you to become a dog trainer, and it especially doesn't mean that you're a really good dog trainer. You need to show potential clients that you have the knowledge and skill set that is required to train their dogs. The more education you have, the higher-quality training you will be able to provide.

Don't forget that you'll be working with the public.

With the above being said, love for dogs is crucial in this business (duh!) but so is the ability to communicate with those on the other end of the leash. You aren't just training canines; you are also teaching their owners. Customer service skills are vital when teaching Fido's other-half how to use commands and other tactics appropriately. Sometimes, it can be even harder than teaching a dog...

Remember that not everyone will have the same amount of knowledge that you do, so you can't expect dog owners to know anything about training animals. Cut them some slack and develop a good sense of patience. Making dog owners feel competent and understanding their needs and concerns is what will set you apart from other trainers in the business. Customer service is a huge part of a thriving business, and those who want to learn how to start a dog training business should look for some good examples, like Amazon or Johnson & Johnson whose love for customers is absolutely top-notch.

If you are articulate and know what you're doing, and you're easy to understand, then chances are good that you have what it takes to launch a successful career as a dog trainer. If you feel like your people skills could use some work, consider investing in a training program. It may sound silly now, but a few night classes in customer service and how to effectively work with clients may be all it takes to make or break your business.

Although it is not uncommon to see dog training companies operate in remote and sparsely populated parts of the country, it is wise for a first-time business owner to find an area where the most people and dogs are. If you are in a market where you could only train an average of 30 dogs a year, then it would be more like a hobby and less like a viable business. This part is called market research, and it's responsible for about half of your success. It's absolutely vital that you do your market research.

Another duh: in order to support and scale your dog training business, you need to be sure that you are opening in the area where there is a high percentage of dog owners. The denser the dog population, the better! According to the American Veterinary Medical Association (AVMA), 36.5% of

U.S. households own a dog, and you want to be near as many of those families as possible.

If you're open to relocation across the country, then focus on settling your business in a state, city and neighborhood where a large number of families own dogs. You can get this information from local animal control officials, town offices, or any other institution that provides information on the number of registered dogs in the area. Also, check the information in surrounding towns, because some people may be likely to travel in order to receive the best service possible (yours!)

After you have thoroughly researched your market and figured out where the demand is, you can start the next step scouting for a location.

"Can I just rent any vacant building for my dog business?"

Yes, of course you can. And you can also save some money by starting in your own house, but there are a few aspects of this plan that need to be considered.

Before choosing the actual physical space where your dog training business will be located, you need to keep this important part in mind: seriously consider (and calculate) how much space in square feet you'll require. This is where many aspiring trainers fail by skimping on space, because usually, successful dog training businesses need plenty of room to move and run. Alternatively, some canine trainers who are learning how to start a dog training business will often begin their entrepreneurial venture in their homes. There's nothing wrong with that if your house is big and has plenty of room where you can accomplish all necessary tasks.

So whether you'd like to run your business out of your home or you're planning on renting a space, make sure it has adequate room for all the supplies and equipment you will need, as well as plenty of space for you and the dogs to move freely while working together.

You also need to think about how easy it is for customers to access your building. If you are planning on running your dog training business out of your home and it's located on a muddy dirt road that is 5 miles from the nearest main road, that's not very easily accessible for your future clientele. You want your business to be easy to find and easy to get to. This is a type of business that highly relies on easy access to location on a daily basis.

Other things to consider when looking for the proper venue when you're just beginning to learn how to start a dog training business are:

- Is there adequate parking?
- Does the location promote the desired image of your business?
- Is there room for future growth?
- Is there competition located near this location?

* Tip: Be sure to check zoning requirements for the city beforehand to make sure you can run a business in that location.

Let's say you have succeeded in locating an area with a large population of dog owners. Chances are that if there are dogs around, there are also well-established pet businesses in the area, possibly even schools and trainers. It is important for your business to stand out by offering something unique, that perhaps the other trainers don't offer. To understand your competition a little better, check and see how far in advance other dog trainers in your target market are booked.

This type of information is necessary to determine whether there is a shortage or over saturation of dog training services in your target area. There will be places where every dog trainer in town can see you today, which probably means there is an excess supply of canine trainers in that area.

If the latter is the case, don't give up yet first, examine your ability to stand out from the competition. Having something special to offer, such as really high-quality training at a lower price with amazing customer service and gifts for dogs (etc.) might be all you need to have your dog training business succeed and grow.

Another thing to consider is the type of training that the other programs are offering. If they use a punishment-based training method, a positive reinforcement method may be exactly what that particular area and its dog owners are looking for. The bottom line is to make sure that the market you are looking to come into isn't over-saturated, or that there's something unique or improved you can offer that hasn't been offered yet.

However, if you've done your research and it seems that there is an abundance of highly-qualified trainers in the area that specialize in the same type of training that you will be offering, it may be time to reconsider your location. Even if you have to commute a few towns over, it will be worth it if there is a chance you will get more business. This type of commitment is what it takes to run a successful dog business.

Now is the time for paperwork

Once you've chosen the perfect location, you're well on your way to understanding how to start a dog training business. Now comes the tedious part – paperwork. A big part of learning how to start a dogtraining business is hidden away in bureaucracy, something many aspiring petpreneurs forget to consider.

The first thing you'll need to do is choose a name for your business. You want it to be something that is catchy and easy for costumers to remember. Before you settle on a name, think about how you'll market your business and make sure that the name is professional looking and great for marketing, too.

Once you've selected the perfect name, it's time to legalize your business. If you're unsure of how to do this, go to your state's business website and do some research. Most states require all businesses to be registered with the state and many have certain licensing regulations as well.

If you can't find all the information that you need online, make a phone call to the state business department and get your questions answered. You don't want to get close to opening your dog training business and realize that you don't have a required license, or worse – get shut down after opening because you didn't file the required paperwork.

You're also going to need insurance. Finding business insurance can be tricky, so shop around well and long. You want to make sure that you have plenty of coverage because you never know what can happen. What if one of the dogs you are training gets hurt and the owners want to blame on you? Same goes for your location – your building/office/area or whatnot needs to be covered in the event there is a fire, flood, etc.

Be smart about your business insurance. At first, focus on the most essential things you'll need and try to minimize your expenses as much as you can. Let's say you live in a place like the desert of Arizona, then flood insurance may not be a high priority for you. Likewise, if you live in Maine you probably won't need tornado coverage.

Talk with multiple different insurance agents and especially read a lot online about all offers you can get before you choose which one to work with. Ensure that your pet business insurance company is giving you the coverage you need without any hidden policies that your business won't require. It's easy to get upsold ten times over your budget.

Now that all your paperwork is completed, you need to keep it organized and in a safe place. You're going to need to refer to this information many times, so you don't want to lose it or have to hunt for it when the time comes. It's never a bad idea to scan everything into your computer so you have a back up copy if you happen to misplace anything.

Hopefully you've been planning on purchasing A LOT of professional dog supplies, because you're going to need them. Talk to other dog trainers, research information online, and come up with a list of all the materials that you will need to run a successful dog training business.

Luckily, Top Dog Tips specializes in profiling dog supplies companies, start-ups and providing reviews on all types of dog products. Read everything on this site to educate yourself on what you need, what you don't need and how to work those things. Obviously you'll need a lot of good quality supplies for training and working with your clientele dogs. Some very first things to consider are:

1. Kennels
2. Clickers
3. Collars
4. Leashes
5. Dog bowls
6. Toys
7. Agility training equipment
8. Treats
9. Calming aids
10. Books and videos
11. General dog training equipment

You'll wear many different hats as a business owner, so don't forget about the other dog products that you'll be needing as well. Think about the office supplies you'll need, too. I'm not just talking about pens, paper, and sticky notes. You'll need that stuff as well but take into account (as an expense) other, much larger and more expensive things.

Obviously, a computer will be necessary to send emails, keep up with your website and social media pages, create invoices, keep records, and much more. You may also need a separate phone line and maybe an answering machine. What about a desk, office chair, and chairs for your clients? The more detailed you make your list now, the more prepared you will be.

Once you have the list down, start restructuring in terms of priority. Every successful business owner should be good at prioritizing stuff. Find ways to spend as least funds as possible in the beginning without sacrificing quality of your services.

Chances are you're not going to have lots of money to hire a cleaning service, general contractor, lawyer, accountant, marketing firm, or web designer at first. In order to keep your start-up costs low, it is advisable to do some of these things yourself. If you don't know how, take a class or find someone who can help you pro-bono.

Do your own painting and household repairs and learn accounting, basic bookkeeping, the basics of online marketing, social media and website design, or at least website maintenance. Doing these simple tasks on your own can help your business get off to a better financial start because your start-up costs will be considerably cheaper. And, if the business fails, you will significantly reduce the impact on your own financial health.

Also, learning everything first-hand will make you a much better boss later down the road once you start outsourcing tasks and hiring professionals to handle specific parts of your dog training business.

Now that you understand how to start a dog training business, the rest is up to you.

Even with a well-prepared plan, starting a dog training business – or ANY business for that matter – isn't easy. There's a lot involved both physically and emotionally, and it can take some time for you to build up a clientele. Try looking online for free resources and visit your local government to look into the rules regarding licensing and registration.

Research the web for financial grants and free business-planning services. There are great benefits to be had from incubator and mentorship programs, along with other government-run services. You'll find resources on creating a dog training business plan and securing financing. Here are just a few of the great resources out there:

BPlans has tons of great stuff to get your business up and running quickly.

Check out MyOwnBusiness for some great free business planning information.

The U.S. Small Business Administration is a great place for info.

Entrepreneur.com has lots of free advice, tips and inspiration.

Remember that everything takes time, and building up a strong business is no exception. Don't expect things to take off right out of the gate. Give yourself time to build relationships with clients and get people in the community talking about your business. Before you know it, you'll have a successful dog training business.

Dog Trainer Certification: Guide for Newbies

one of the most rewarding jobs for those who enjoy interacting with both people and dogs is being a dog trainer. But how does one go about embarking on this career path and acquiring dog trainer certification without any experience? We've got the answer right here.

Prior to looking into a dog trainer's class, it is important to do a little research and study the industry to make sure that this is the profession best suited for your personality. While it is not mandated to have a dog trainer certification to actually start training canines for money, it is highly recommended. Certification proves that you are dedicated to this field and know exactly what you're doing (plus, it makes the job hunting slightly easier).

Below you'll find the what, how, when and where on all the questions related to becoming a professional dog trainer and getting your dog trainer certification, even if you're a complete newbie in this field.

Before we begin, it's important to point out the difference between dog trainer's certificate and dog trainer certification, because the two are not the same.

Dog trainer's certificate. When you embark on the journey of getting your Dog Trainer Certificate, this is an educational program that will teach you all the necessary skills on how to train dogs as a professional, work with clients and in dog training schools.

There are dog trainer certificate courses, and the end of which you do receive a certificate. However, this doesn't mean that you're 100% qualified to train canines professionally, and this certificate won't carry too much weight on your resume to tip the scale in your favor when looking for a job.

Dog trainer certification. Certification is an actual examination of your knowledge, experience and skills in the industry and training dogs as a professional. In America, there is only one truly serious organization (CCPDT) that can truly assess your suitability for this profession and certify you as a qualified dog trainer. They will determine if you meet all the necessary criteria and in order to maintain your status, you will also need to continue your education as a professional dog trainer with your choosen school.

Note: Not all certifications are the same, so do your research well – read reviews, talk to people, browse online through websites like APDT's database, etc. Also, remember to always distinguish between a certification with a private dog training school (-no-) and an independent certifying body (-yes-).

Below, we've made a quick checklist of things to do if you feel like dog training is the profession for you and that is something you would like to continue developing your skills in.

To-do list before you get dog trainer certification

1. Research animal behavior science. It is important to understand dog's cognitive functions, psychology, how an animal learns new

things and so forth simply to be able to create a training program of your own. When researching articles on this subject, remember to be skeptical and engage your critical thinking skills. Because of how this information can affect your future career and the canines you'll be working with, ensure the books and articles you read are written by accredited professionals in the field and not self proclaimed "dog experts."

2. Read as many books about dog training as you can. There are numerous books on dog ownership, on dog training and on acquiring dog trainer certification written by actual dog trainers and other professionals with strong credentials. If you're not looking to buy any of these, get to your local library and start there; read a lot on what it really means to be a professional dog trainer and what this occupation entails.

3. Get to know your local dog shelters. One of the best ways to become comfortable with interacting with dogs and people is to volunteer at your local animal shelter(s). Not only are you able to spend time with dogs on a daily basis, but you are presented a chance to practice what you may already know and learn how to tweak your dog training and communication skills. It's a great way to be around a larger group of unfamiliar canines and find ways of how to properly handle them.

4. Check out local training schools. Alternatively, you can also volunteer at dog training schools, but those are more difficult to get into. If you're not accepted as a volunteer, enroll your dog into an obedience training class so you can get the feel for what it's like to be a client of a trainer. Additionally, some canine training schools will allow you to come in and observe how a training

class goes, and you can notice the way each dog trainer handles certain situations. Look up to those dog trainers whose methods you like the most, who promote solid positive-reinforcement training and have a great rapport with their clients.

5. Find any other ways to get experience. Aside from trying to get your big break with the help of dog training schools and animal shelters, try to convince your friends or family that you're qualified enough (even without dog trainer certification on your hands yet) to train their dogs. Establish your own base of clientele, even if you have just a couple of dogs to train on the weekends. The important part is to be able to put down the actual experience on your resume, and have good references for the future.

6. Take dog trainer certification classes. This one goes without saying – if you want to be a

professional, at some point you need to invest into professional training. Additionally, find time to attend dog certification seminars, which will normally be held by your local animal shelters or dog training schools. The reason these are useful is because they are geared towards dog owners, which expands your knowledge base on how to train pet owners themselves on performing commands for their own dogs.

7. Start your search for a place of work early. Once you have a firm grasp on training and have acquired your dog trainer certification, start looking for canine training schools or animal shelters that are hiring. Truth be told, it's not easy to get hired when you don't have strong credentials, so you might need to follow the advice listed below. Nevertheless, when looking to apply your newly acquired dog trainer certification mastery, always ask questions as to

how professionals there train dogs and compare if this matches with what you've learned and/or what you're comfortable with. New place of work has to be a good fit both ways.

8. A lot of dog trainers start out as apprentices. As with many other trades, this is a great way to learn the ins and outs of your future career under someone who has been doing it for a long time. Even if you have already acquired your dog trainer certification, this will give you an opportunity to see how a real dog training class goes and start applying some of your knowledge. While these positions are non-paid or very low paid, it's still a great start if you are unsure of your dog training abilities and wish for more experience and hands-on training. Depending on the dog trainer you will be working with as an apprentice, it could take more than 6 months of teaching alongside him before you are ready to

venture out on your own. Once you feel you know what you're in terms of training dogs by yourself, and you understand the essence of how this business works – it's time to proceed onto the next big step of your dog trainer's career, and that is your official dog trainer's certificate.

9. Get your dog trainer certification. There are multiple places in America where you can become officially certified as a professional dog trainer (listed below). You will need to provide proof of your experience, dog training classes, dog certification classes and take exams. But once you're done with this step, you can consider yourself as a professional (who's probably still out of work), and you are already more certified to train canines than half of other dog trainers in the country who never took the professional training route. This will give you a boost when looking for a job.

10. Don't stop educating yourself. Your must always continue to hone your dog training skills and continue your education and expanding your knowledge of being a professional dog trainer. Also, remember that once you have received your dog trainer certification, it is actually required for you to take continuing canine training education classes to maintain your status as an officially certified trainer. **Schools that prepare you to be a dog trainer**

More often than not, you don't need any specific school/course to become a dog trainer – majority of dog trainers are self-taught and used the methods we've outlined above in the checklist. What matters is getting the dog trainer certification, which proves that you truly are knowledgeable in the subject as well as experienced. What methods you used do not matter as much as long as the result is "qualified."

That being said, there's an extremely huge amount of dog trainer's schools in the US; most of those courses are provided by the same schools that train dogs and supposedly will hire you if you complete their training (which is not the case more often than not, unfortunately). The best way is to use Google search with a keyword of your city, and check out local training schools if your heart is set on going this way.

- Remember that a good dog trainer's school should focus on the following topics:
- Canine behavior and psychology
- General animal learning
- Dog training history
- Dog training class design

You will go through lectures (online or in the school), reading assignments and practical hands-on experience of training canines. To put it simply, if you can afford this course and have time to spend as well – go for it! Just don't put all of your eggs in one basket and do not consider yourself a well-qualified trainer who will be hired immediately simply because you finished private training school's course. Your next step should still be to get a CCPDT dog trainer certification (read below).

Schools that prepare for dog trainer certification

APDT - Dog Trainer Certification: A Guide for NewbiesJust as there are plenty of schools for dog trainer's, there's also a lot of schools that can prepare you for dog trainer certification. In fact, there are so many of them that it's pointless to list even just a few (most likely you'll want to attend your local school).

The best way to go about this is to use APDT's search and database of designations for dog trainer certification schools:

Certifications On the APDT Trainer Search

In addition, you can also use APDT's courses and resources to prepare yourself for the exam. Association of Professional Dog Trainers (APDT) is a professional organization of dog trainers that offers an annual conference with hands-on canine training with live animals. There are also multi-week online classes with lectures, discussion boards and homework offered by APDT.

Also, if you simply want to brush up on your dog training skills, or are curious about certain canine training topics, you can also gain access to their database of webinars which are done by dog training professionals from all over the world. It's well worth it.

CPDT - Dog Trainer Certification: A Guide for NewbiesTo receive your dog trainer certification, get in touch with Certification Council for Professional Dog Trainers (CCPDT). Once you have taken the above listed steps in the checklist and feel ready to start your new career as a dog trainer, know that there will be additional tasks to accomplish before you become certified.

According to the Certification Council for Professional Dog Trainers, to become certified by them, you need to have at least 300 hours of training experience and recommendations from those you have trained with. This is is where your hard work and experience with friends' dogs, volunteering in dog shelters and training schools as well as working as an apprentice will pay off.

After you can provide that to CCPDT, you are required to take an exam to demonstrate the knowledge you have received during your training, experience and dog certification classes. If you choose to go through the Certification Council for Professional Dog Trainers, know that they come very highly recommended in the industry. CCPDT's certificate is a national dog trainer certification and the only one that actually carries some weight, while most other ones will not look as impressive on your resume.

Note: Alternatively, you can also try to get certified with International Association of Animal Behavior Consultants (IAABC); however, we cannot comment on this organization as we're unsure on how big of an impact dog trainer certification issued by IAABC can have on your career (you might want to research this group, or simply go with CCPDT).

Depending on what area you want to focus on, as already mentioned above, there are the certifications for becoming a dog trainer, but you can also venture into becoming a therapy dog trainer.

ADI - Dog Trainer Certification: A Guide for NewbiesAssistance Dogs International (ADI) has a ton of information on how to train therapy dogs. But before you decide to delve deep into this complicated area of canine training, be prepared for a really tough challenge as well as at least a 10 year commitment.

Dog therapy training goes well beyond just teaching an owner how to train their dog; it is about being able to match a therapy dog with a client in need. Unlike regular dog training, it can take anywhere from 2-3 years of apprenticeship to become a therapy dog trainer, and it can take over 6 months to train a single dog. Training a therapy dog is very time consuming and does require a large long-term commitment, but in the end, it can very rewarding. You can contact Assistance Dogs International organization for finding a local program; they're very helpful in that regard.

Getting back on the subject of your regular dog trainer certification, be prepared that it will be a challenge to find a job in this field because it's very competitive. Be ready to brush up your researching skills and apply them in your local area to find places for experience, volunteering, apprenticeships, schools, training, certificates and, finally – a steady job.

Becoming a dog trainer – either a regular one or training therapy dogs – can be very a rewarding and fun career. With the right training and knowledge, you can go a long way in this exciting adventure. Possibly even open your own training school eventually, and become the next Cesar Millan?

A Sample Dog Training Business Plan Template

Are you about starting a dog training center? If YES, here is a complete sample dog training business plan template & feasibility report you can use for FREE.

Okay, so we have considered all the requirements for starting a dog training business. We also took it further by analyzing and drafting a sample dog training service marketing plan template backed up by actionable guerrilla marketing ideas for dog training businesses. So let's proceed to the business planning section.

According to statistics, the United States of America has more than 77.5 million dogs, with the number projected to grow each year. This has also caused an increase in demand for dog training services. States such as New York and California have a large number of dogs and dog owners and so this makes it a thriving place for dog training businesses.

Data from the American Pet Product Association stated as at 2012, that those who spent on their pets in the United States of America, climbed to a new record revenue level of $53 billion dollars. Pet services, according to data of which dog training is a part of, generated $4.4 billion dollars in 2012, and the projection for the next several years shows a positive gain.

According to a 2015 survey, 65% of households in the United States of America own at least a pet, these amounts to over 300 million pets that need to be cared and catered for. The pet industry on its own has products and services (training, food, daycare, medical services, toys, and a whole lot of other services) on ground so as to keep these pets healthy, alive and happy.

Pets are being owned by all economic levels of households in the United States of America; however, households with higher incomes accounted for about 60% of the total money spent on pets. Data from the American Pet Products Association (APPA) has revenue in the pet industry to be projected at $62.75 billion in 2016, which is an increase of over 4% from that of 2015. Since 2002, the average growth rate annually has been 5.4% and the revenue has been steadily growing over the last two decades.

The Bureau of Labor Statistics (BLS) has states that the job growth for the pet industry is expected to be above average as it had been experiencing 11% growth from 2014 which was expected to last till 2024. Also, revenue for pet services grew from $5.41 billion in 2015 to $5.73 billion in 2016.

Baby boomers are not only spending on their pets according to statistics but pampering them as well. It has been found that spending for pets has peaked between the ages of 55 and 64. Also, millennials (those born between 1985 – 2010) who have disposable income are also spending for and spoiling their pets. The pet industry has continued to grow even during major economic downturns, which shows that the industry has a huge advantage over others.

Executive Summary

Woofy Dog Training Services is a standard dog training business in San Francisco – California, USA and intends to ensure that customers who owned dogs are offered training services as well as other services, such as dog sitting, grooming and so on for their dogs.

We also intend to offer consultancy and advisory services to those who intend to start the business but do not possess the know-how. Our vision is to ensure that we become the preferred dog training service here in San Francisco – California and also the top six dog training business in the whole United States of America by 2020.

To attain our vision and objectives, we have ensured that only the best professionals = from management staff to the low end staff – have been hired by us. This shows how willing we are to go the extra mile in ensuring that we lay a solid foundation in our business structure.

Our staff will not only be the best paid employees across the industry amongst similar start-ups, but they will also undergo training and performance appraisals to ensure that their skills as well as their productivity are enhanced. We know how important having a good location that is convenient for our customers is and so we have chosen a very strategic location that is not only convenient for our customers but also our employees as well.

We abhor cruelty to animals and indeed pets and so we will ensure that we hold ourselves and employees to that standard of not applying cruelty to the dogs in which we will be training. Also, we believe in achieving customer excellence and due to this, we intend to train our customer care executives in the act of answering and handling our customers – the dog owners.

While Bill Trump holds a Doctorate degree in Certified Applied Animal Behavior with clinical work for the past 10 years focused on behavioral problems in dogs; his wife Maggie holds a Masters in Business Administration from a prestigious school. The two who love dogs also have several dog training certifications and experience in this industry, and will therefore bring their experience and expertise to bear in this business.

Our Products and Services

Woofy Dog Training Service is an established dog training service that intends to offer all our customers and their dogs varied services in a bid to make their experience at our company a delightful one.

The reason why we intend to offer other services in addition to our main service is so as not to be able to attract more customers in our target market to our business but also boost our sources of income thereby ensuring that we have a healthy bottom line. Our offering of other services will however be in line with the permissible laws of the United States of America. Therefore some of the products and services we intend to offer are:

- Boarding kernel
- Groomers
- Doggie day care
- Dog walkers
- Pet sitters
- Dog show handlers
- Pet taxi
- Pooper Scooper
- Pet boutique
- Consultancy and advisory services
- Franchises

Our Vision Statement

Our vision is to be the preferred dog trainer in California and amongst the top six dog training business in United States of America by 2020.

Our Mission Statement

Our mission is to ensure that we will meet the demands and preferences of our customers by offering different services in our dog training business for our various customers here in California.

Business Structure

No matter how low scaled a business is, having the right business structure is very important, and so at Woofy Dog Training Service, we are committed to ensuring that we get it right from the beginning by hiring employees who are not only dedicated and hard working to handle all the various positions in our company, but also committed to the company's true vision and objectives.

Because we want only what's best for Woofy Dog Training Services, we are ready to ensure that we not only correctly source the right individuals for the different available positions but that we also pay the right amount that will not only keep them committed but also improve their productivity and invariably boost out bottom line.

- We intend to ensure that our management staff are those with vast experience and have the required knowledge that is necessary to ensure that we attain our goals and objectives and also be able to communicate these values not only to the employees under them but also to customers of Woofy Dog Training Services as well. Therefore, below is the business structure we intend building for Woofy Dog Training Services;
- Chief Executive Officer
- Admin and Human Resource Manager
- Dog Trainer Supervisor

- Marketing Team
- Accountants/Cashiers
- Customer Service Executives
- Purchasing Manager
- Security Guard
- Driver
- Cleaners
- Roles and Responsibilities

Chief Executive Officer

1. In charge of making strategic decisions on behalf of the company
2. Drafts and ensures company policies are understood and implemented by the employees
3. Evaluates the success of Woofy Dog Training Service
4. Admin and Human Resource Manager
5. In charge of recruiting competent employees on behalf of the company

6. Reviews employees work rate by carrying out regular performance appraisals
7. Ensures that the administration of the company runs smoothly

Dog Trainer Supervisor

1. In charge of all the dog trainers in the facility
2. Reviews dog training methods and changes ineffective or inappropriate ones
3. Remains updated about happenings in the industry for the benefit of the company

Marketing Team

1. Responsible for conducting market research that will identify new target market
2. Drafts and implements marketing strategies on behalf of organization
3. Promotes the company via its social media platforms and official website

Accountants/Cashiers

1. In charge of invoices and dispensing cash to be used within the office
2. Prepares financial statements and records on behalf of the company
3. Ensures that tax is adequately prepared and submitted to the tax authorities

Customer Service Executives

1. In charge of answering customers' enquiries and resolving complaints
2. Keeps and updates an accurate customer database on behalf of the company
3. Carries out any other duty as might be determined by the Human resources manager

Purchasing Manager

1. In charge of ensuring adequate supplies of items at Woofy Dog Training Services

2. Liaises with reliable vendors and distributors and keeps a mutually satisfying relationship with them

3. Prepares and reviews contracts for vendors and suppliers

Security Guard

1. Ensures that all within the premises – people and property – are safe during work hours

2. Keeps guard over facility after work hours

3. Driver

4. Conducts all the ferrying of the dogs to and fro the facility

5. Carries out light maintenance on vehicle and reports major faults to appropriate quarters

6. Carries out any other duties as might be determined by the Human resources manager

Cleaner

1. Ensures that the facility is kept hygienically clean at all times
2. Ensures that the rest rooms are kept neat for visitors and employees
3. Carries out any other duties as determined by the Human Resources manager

SWOT Analysis

Due to our need to start off on the right foundation, we got the best consultant here in California who had an experience of this industry to look through our business concept and determine if it was worth the time and effort we were willing to put into it.

To ensure that the results were accurate enough, our consultant made use of the SWOT (Strength, Weakness, Opportunities, and Threats) analysis to determine if the business was worth going into and if we were likely to succeed going into the business. Below is the preview of the results from the SWOT Analysis that were conducted on behalf of Woofy Dog Training Service:

Strengths

Our strength lies in the fact that we will be offering our customers other services in addition to our core service – dog training so as to be able to meet up with our customers varying needs whilst also attracting more customers to our business.

Another factor that is to our advantage is that we have well qualified staff that will ensure that the business attains its original goals and objectives here in California as well as the whole of the United States of America. Another huge strength in our favor is the husband and wife tea, Bill and

Maggie Trump who are dog lovers and have several certifications as well as years of business.

Weakness

California is a city after New York, where there are a lot of dog owners and dogs, which means that there are enough dog training services here in California making the market seem saturated and posing a challenge for us who intend to make an impact into this business. Regardless of the fact that our location might be our weakness, we are confident that grand opening party will pave the way for us to penetrate and grab a fair share of the market.

Opportunities

The opportunities available to us as a business intending to make an impression are limitless as we intend to continually re-innovate our services so as to differentiate us from other dog training services. Also, we intend to offer consultancy and advocacy services as well as franchises for those who intend to start up newly in this business and have no inkling what to do.

Threats

The threats we are likely to face while starting or running a dog training business are, liability as the dogs might damage property while undergoing training; new competitors are likely to crop up in our location making it more difficult for us to hold onto our market share as they will compete with us for a share of the market.

Another threat is an economic downturn that will likely affect how dog owners spend on their dogs. As a business, we are aware of the fact that threats will crop up but we are also confident and optimistic that our laid down proactive strategies will combat any threat that might likely occur.

Market Trends

Generally, this business is one that can be started with low capital as money for overhead is very low. Generally trainers rarely have a physical location to operate their dog training business; instead they travel to the homes of clients or go to boarding facilities for dogs in order to provide their services.

Also, asides from not needing to rent a physical location in which to start the business, there is also little investment that is needed in order to buy the equipment necessary to ensure that the business is being run efficiently. If you need to acquire any extra equipment at all, this might include a few extra leashes, dog treats, clickers as well as other aids that can assist in training the dogs.

Another trend is on the pricing structure where dog training rates are usually within same range in the same location, so as to make it easier to compete. However, those who tended to offer special discounted rates or give out a free session were those who were new trainers and did that in order to attract clients and grow the business.

Also, the rates for dog trainers usually fall in between the half-hourly and hourly rates especially when it is a private lesson. The rates are also lowered for group training classes.

Finally, the last trend is the use of the internet, which has been used as a major tool of penetrating the market and attracting new customers from the target market, whilst also communicating the core values of the brand via publicity through its social media platforms.

Dog training services especially those that operated from home knows how powerful deploying the internet effectively can be. Furthermore, , dog trainers' network with kernel boarding facilities, pet boutiques and groomers, so as to be able to source for clients for their dog training business.

Our Target Market

Even though plenty households in the United States of America own dogs as pet and California and New York are amongst states where the highest owners of dogs and dogs themselves live, thereby spiking the demand for dog training services in this area; we still however cannot limit our target market to just households, especially here in California.

It is for this reason that we conducted a thorough market research on this industry so as to be able to garner accurate facts and data that would allow us correctly predict what our customers and the target market would be expecting from us, which would allow us better draft strategies that would serve them better. We are therefore in business to offer our dog training services to the following groups of people here in California;

- Households
- Corporate Executives
- Business people
- Celebrities and important personalities
- Sports men and women
- Boarding facilities

Our Competitive Advantage

Our vision when starting Woofy Dog Training service was so that we could be the preferred dog training business here in California and also amongst the top six in the whole United States of America by 2020. To achieve this vision, we know how necessary it is for us to come up with competitive advantage strategies that will stand us apart from other dog training businesses here in California.

First off, we are going to ensure that we offer training services mixed with other dog services for our customers, as this will allow us attract and grab a better share of the target market.

Another competitive strategy is the fact that we have hired the right management staff for our company that are not knowledgeable and have vast experience but one that knows our core values as a business and also knows understands how to bring the business up from scratch to become something to be reckoned with.

We intend to ensure that our customer service executives are adequately trained to handle all our customer's enquiries and complaints and ensure that all are promptly resolved on behalf of the organization. Asides our management staff, we intend to ensure that all our employees are adequately trained, paid and have welfare packages that are the best amongst similar dog training start-ups here in California.

Sources of Income

Woofy Dog Training Service is a business that has been established with the aim of making profit and favorably competing with other such businesses in the pet industry in California and in the United States of America. We intend to offer different services to all the dogs of our various customers here in California as well as all over United States of America.

Therefore the sources of income we intend to generate at Woofy Dog Trainers are:

- Boarding kernel
- Groomers
- Doggie day care
- Dog walkers
- Pet sitters
- Dog show handlers
- Pet taxi
- Pooper Scooper
- Pet boutique
- Consultancy and advisory services
- Franchises

Sales Forecast

According to the American Pet Association, dogs are amongst the top three pets owned by most Americans, which means that demand for dog training services will continually surge. California is one of the two top cities that have the most dog owners and dogs, which makes it a good enough place for us to not only generate enough income for our business but also start to make profit that will grow our business from the second year into the business.

The sales projections were done after much critical evaluation conducted by us as well as by a sales expert familiar with this industry. The sales expert was able to come up with this reliable forecast after gathering accurate data from similar start-ups here in California.

Below is the expected sales projection for Woofy Dog Training Services based on present data that is deemed reliable:

First Fiscal Year-: $200,000

Second Fiscal Year-: $400,000

Third Fiscal Year-: $800,000

N.B: It should be noted that the above projections were done with available data and information that was obtained from the pet industry at the time and that was deemed accurate. The projections were done on the assumptions that the love and ownership for dogs would not decline, there won't be any major competitors and that there won't be a major economic meltdown to warrant customers not having enough to spend extra for their dogs. Any change in the above factors is likely to affect the sales projections figures to go up or down.

Marketing Strategy and Sales Strategy

Marketing is a very important aspect of any business as it does the purpose of ensuring that money is generated for the business whilst also creating awareness for the business. However, to be able to draft effective marketing strategies for Woofy Dog Training Services, we intend to first conduct a critical and thorough marketing survey that will allow us best understand the market we intend going into and how best we would penetrate it.

Carrying out this market survey required us sourcing and getting reliable and detailed data so as to get an accurate result from our market survey, which will allow us compete against other dog training service businesses here in California.

To help us in conducting this market research, we hired a marketing expert who is not only reputable but has a deep understanding of the pet industry and what it would take to be able to penetrate the target market for customers who owned and cared for their dogs. The expert has already come up with strategies that will allow us get a large percentage of the market here in California.

Also, our marketing tea have not been out of the picture, as they have been empowered to draft, modify or review and implement effective marketing strategies to sell our services as well as products on behalf of Woofy Dog Training Service.

Marketing has however evolved digitally due to changing times, as few people are relying less on the word of mouth direct marketing and instead using the search engine or social media platforms to make their findings. And so, if you are looking to survive in this new age, you will need to ensure that you build a website for your dog training business and also get an Search Engine Optimization (SEO) expert to help you with ensuring that your website pops up on search engine when people are searching for anything related to dog training service.

Therefore, at Woofy Dog Training Service intends to adopt the following marketing and sales approach towards selling our products and services;

Word-of-mouth or direct marketing

Launching of a website with unique colors and logos to market our dog training services

Place ads in local newspapers and magazines as well as on radio and television stations here in California

Print fliers and distribute it in target areas to dog owners and lovers

Network with dog walkers and veterinary clinics to get information about potential clients

Ask customers for reciprocal referrals and give discounts for those who do

Start our business with a huge bang by throwing a dog costume themed party for dog and in extension pet owners here in California so as to create awareness

Leverage on social media platforms such as Facebook, Twitter and Instagram to market our dog training services

Ensure that our dog training business is listed in local directories

Dog Training Business Plan – Publicity and Advertising Strategy

No matter what kind of business one intends to go into, ensuring that one drafts and implements effective publicity and advertising strategy is very important. Also, offering publicity for our Woofy Dog Training Services will ensure that we are able to not only attract the intended customers we seek but also to compete favorably against other competitors in the market place.

There are several things that boosts the success chances of a publicity strategy and we at Woofy Dog Training Services intends to exploit these factors for the benefit of our company here in California and so as to be able to achieve our vision and objectives in the United States of America by 2020. We also intend to combine several factors in ensuring that we publicize and advertise our dog training business successfully.

Below are the publicity and advertising strategies we intend to use in promoting and communicating our Woofy Dog Training Business to customers.

Sending out newsletters and coupons to customers – existing and potential

Print business cards with relevant information and logo and distribute in relevant areas

Place adverts in local newspapers, magazines as well as on local radio and television stations

Attend dog fairs and events and create awareness for Woofy Dog Training Services

Sponsor dog events and other related dog programs in local community

Distribute our fliers in target locations and also paste in legal conspicuous places

Ensure that we print customized tee-shirts for all our employees here at Woofy Dog Training Services

Our Pricing Strategy

Before deciding on the pricing strategy for our dog training business, we would need to conduct a thorough market research on what other dog training centers are offering their customers. Normally, trainers usually offer rates depending on the services required from customers, and so we would ensure that we offer various packages that would require different rates for our customers.

However, because we are just starting this business newly, we intend to offer prices that were slightly lower than that of our competitors in the first six months of business. Our lower rates will however still be within comparable range of existing businesses so that we do not run our business at a loss. We have carried out a detailed strategy and seen that this will encourage more customers to patronize our business.

Payment Options

Woofy Dog Training Services intends to operate a payment policy that will suit all our different customers and whatever paying options they might prefer in paying for services offered them by our company. Therefore, the payment options we intend to offer our various customers are;

- Cash payment
- Payment via credit card
- Payment via check
- Payment via Point of Sale (POS) Machine

The above payment option platforms were carefully chosen by our bank for our target market, and we have been assured that the platforms will run without any hitches.

Start – Up Expenditure (Budget)

Even though the dog training business is not seen as a capital intensive business for any entrepreneur that wants to go into such business, it still however needs to generate capital to be successfully operational in its first few months of business and sort overhead expenses especially if it intends to rent a facility and employ staff as well as pay certain utility bills that will be incurred during the process of running the business.

Therefore the key areas where we intend to spend our start-up capital on at Woofy Dog Training Services include;

Fee for registering the business here in the United States of America – $750

Licenses and permits, accounting software as well as other legal expenses incurred during the registration process – $1250

Cost of hiring a business consultant – $2,000

Insurance coverage (General liability, property insurance, and workers' compensation) – $4,000

Cost of purchasing start-up equipment in bulk (such as leashes, clickers, dog treats as well as other dog aid training materials) – $10,000

Cost of leasing and renovating a facility for dog training business for at least a year – $33,000

Marketing and publicity expenses (for grand opening party as well as normal business operations) – $5,000

Operational cost for the first six months of running the business (employee salaries, payment of bills) – $100,000

Other start-up expenses which includes furniture, stationeries, phone, and computer – $5,500

Cost of purchasing an official vehicle – $30,000

Cost of launching a website – $500

Cost of throwing a grand opening party – $3,000

Other miscellaneous expenses – $5,000

From the above calculations, we would need an estimate of $200,000 if we intend to fully start and successfully run our dog training business here in California. It should be noted that the half of the start-up capital will be used to pay the salaries of our employees as well as pay certain utility bills that would be incurred during the months of operation.

Generating Funding / Startup Capital for Woofy Dog Training Business

Woofy Dog Training Services is a business owned and run by husband and wife, Bill and Maggie Trump. This is a family business and as such we do not intend to have any external partner which is the major reason why our sources of generating capital have been limited to three.

Therefore the areas which we intend to source for capital for our dog training business are:

Generate part of start-up capital from personal savings

Sourcing for soft loan from wealthy family members and friends

Applying for loan from the bank

N.B: From our personal savings, we were able to generate the sum of about $30,000. The soft loans from our wealthy friends and family members amounted to $40,000. We approached the bank several months bank for a loan of $130,000 and after submitting several paper works; we have not only been approved for a loan but the amount will at any moment from now be credited to our business account.

Sustainability and Expansion Strategy

Establishing a business whose intention is to make profit and compete favorably with its competitors is just one aspect of running a business, ensuring that the business is sustained and even expanded later is another aspect that requires certain strategies, such as employees' competence, customer loyalty as well as well as re-innovation of services strategies.

Any business that wants to remain in existence for a long time has to see to it that they employ staffs that are competent and knowledgeable enough about the business' objectives to be able to bring it to fruition. This is why it is very important that we employ only the best hands for our dog training services from the management staff down to our trainers and other low end staff.

We intend to not only pay our workers well but also continually see to it that they undergo training every now and then that will not only enhance their skill but improve productivity for the company as well. Another aspect we intend to look into whilst implementing our sustainability and expansion strategies include ensuring that we keep our customers happy and satisfied with our services as this will ensure that they remain loyal to us.

We will continually improve on the services we offer our clients and will endeavor to listen to and act on feedback. We will also give our loyal customers discounts for every referral they bring our way, this way; we seal our customers' loyalty to us.

Finally, we intend to ensure that our services are continually reviewed and re-innovated as this will ensure that we continue to have an edge over our competitors. With these ways, we are sure that we will comfortably be able to sustain and then expand our own business at our own pace.

Check List / Milestone

Business Name Availability Check: Completed

Business Registration: Completed

Opening of Corporate Bank Accounts: Completed

Securing Point of Sales (POS) Machines: Completed

Opening Mobile Money Accounts: Completed

Opening Online Payment Platforms: Completed

Application and Obtaining Tax Payer's ID: In Progress

Application for business license and permit: Completed

Purchase of Insurance for the Business: Completed

Conducting Feasibility Studies: Completed

Generating capital from family members: Completed

Applications for Loan from the bank: In Progress

Writing of Business Plan: Completed

Drafting of Employee's Handbook: Completed

Drafting of Contract Documents and other relevant Legal Documents: In Progress

Design of The Company's Logo: Completed

Graphic Designs and Printing of Packaging Marketing / Promotional Materials: In Progress

Recruitment of employees: In Progress

Creating Official Website for the Company: In Progress

Creating Awareness for the business both online and around the community: In Progress

Health and Safety and Fire Safety Arrangement (License): Secured

Opening party / launching party planning: In Progress

Establishing business relationship with vendors – wholesale suppliers / merchants: In Progress

Purchase of trucks: Completed

Top 21 Must-Know Dog Training Tips

Dogs and people are two very different animals. We can't live without dogs, but then we also can't live with them if they behave like a bona fide animal of the wild. Every passionate dog person loves a trained canine, so here are twenty one dog training tips that every owner should know about.

But first, why do you need to know this?

Even though canines are famous for being a man's best friend, there are just too many tendencies in their behavior that eventually will get annoying for the owner. Most of those dog problems will also hurt your pets themselves, which is one of the primary reasons for dog lovers to attend to them ASAP.

On the other hand, there are things that dog owners themselves love to do (or love not to do), which ultimately annoys or otherwise affects your dog. Those things are just as important to fix, because dog ownership is a two way street – take a little, give a little. Now, let's quickly take a look at what are some the most important and already well-known dog training tips.

Show affection

Begin with the easiest one – show your dog affection. Our loyal friends are social animals, and they appreciate your affection almost always.

Don't notice only the bad things your puppy has done, but remember to also acknowledge their good behavior, preferably every single time.

Focus on your body language

Dogs will easily pickup on all kinds of body language from humans, so you need to be aware of the type of signals you might be sending to your dog.

Learn how your pooch reacts to specific gestures or vocal commands, and use those to train your dog accordingly.

Guide your dog

Always provide your canine with more information than a simple "no!" Remember that your pooch doesn't understand the human language, and "no" is simply a sound-command to them.

Whenever he has done something wrong, screaming "no" at him will tell him that he's done something wrong but he won't know what.

Use things your dog loves

A great way to train your dog effectively is to use his favorite items such as dog toys or maybe an old shoe.

In addition, use other things that your dog might love: petting, affection, a game of fetch, access onto furniture or come home, etc.

Don't over-hype yourself

Remember to have realistic expectations about the accomplishments of your puppy.

Some dogs learn certain things faster, and others might take some more time to be trained. Be patient, and both of you will get there eventually.

Stay consistent

Dog training requires pet owners to put in a lot of hours into this vocation, and be dedicated to achieve the goal.

If you lose sight of where your dog training is going, it will be more difficult for the dog to pick up what you're trying to teach him. And if brakes between session are long, same applies.

Don't mislead your pooch

Be clear about the signals that you send to your dog.

For example, if your dog jumps on you whenever you get home, and you start hugging and encouraging him, then he just learned that people love when he jumps on them, and will pursue this with others.

Keep your pet's health in check

If you're taking your dog's training very seriously with rigorous exercise on a daily basis, you need to remember to occasionally check in with the vet and keep your dog's health in check.

Some things might exhaust them and open up doors for all kinds of illnesses. Regular check ups at your local vet clinic are an important part of owning a dog.

Reward your dog with freedom

Affection is good, but your dog also will appreciate if as he learns new things on his own.

Let them roam free sometimes, experience the world and become aware of what is around them on a daily basis. It's important for canine to get used to the environment and be themselves sometimes.

Give your dogs appropriate names

There's a whole science behind choosing a proper name for your dog.

Research this subject to find out what would be the most optimal way to name your dog so that he reacts well during training, and really understands when you address him with a command.

Listen to what your dog communicates

Be aware and try to see what your dog communicates to you.

By observing your pet, you can notice how they behave around other animals, if they're happy or uncomfortable in certain situations, and similar. Don't force your dogs to do something they're strictly opposed to.

Make home rules very clear

Your canine should know all the house rules from an early age, and be aware of exactly where they can go, where they can sleep and what is out of bounds for them.

This is part of a successful dog training regime and ensures that your dog is obedient at all times.

Know if your dogs like what you feed them

Even if it's the most popular dog food brand, that doesn't mean your dog will be a big fan of that product.

Test it with your pet, see how they react to your dog treat or dog food, and whether they get excited every time you get ready to feed it to them.

Provide your dogs with their own place

It's good when your pet have their own home, a place they know they can go to to hide.

Whether it's a dog house, or dog bed, or a corner with a sleeping pad, it's good to let your puppy know about the place as early as possible and have them get used to it.

Don't let others confuse your dog

If you're not living alone, and there are other family members in the household that communicate with the dog, be sure to let them know on how you decided to train your pet.

If you don't let your dog to sit on the furniture and others allow that, your dog will be confused.

React in a timely manner

Dogs have short memories, so whenever you're training to reinforce their good behavior or otherwise have them connect something to the actions they've done, you need to be quick about it.

When your dog does something positive, reinforce their good behavior immediately.

Provide a generous diet

Don't skimp on dog food, try to provide your pet with the highest quality dog food and a necessary amount of vitamins.

Adopt the diet based on your dog breed's needs as well as based on how active your pet is. Aim for higher protein amount and dog foods with good reviews.

Have fun with your pooch

Training's training, but it's also important to have fun with your dog.

Make time to spend with your canine and play a game of fetch, chase each other or simply be silly for a while and indulge your dog in some active, fun games. It's an important part of successful dog training regime.

Don't forget about dog treats

Stock up on high quality, good and healthy dog treats which you should use to reinforce your dog's good behavior.

This is one of the most optimal ways to train your dog for most things, so learn how to use treats in training your dog and make the best out of it.

Signing up for a class can help

While not completely necessary, it might be interesting and beneficial for both you and your pooch to sign up for some training classes, especially dog agility class.

Your dog will socialize with other canines, as well as well-trained dog professionals. He will get plenty of exercise and learn new things.

Every training session with your dog must end on a positive note.

Pet your dog, let them know that you're happy with what he has done and try to reward them somehow. A tasty dog treat, or a little game with the dog can be a good reward for the dog to understand that it's worth trying.